The Blue Economy and Small States

Commonwealth Blue Economy Series, No. 1

Commonwealth Secretariat

The Commonwealth

Commonwealth Secretariat
Marlborough House
Pall Mall
London SW1Y 5HX
United Kingdom

Published by the Commonwealth Secretariat
Edited by PrePress Projects Ltd
Typeset by NovaTechset Private Limited, Bengaluru & Chennai, India
Cover design by Commonwealth Secretariat
Printed and bound by CPI Group (UK) Ltd, Croydon, CR0 4YY

Prepared by Julian Roberts, Adviser in the Oceans and Natural Resources Advisory Division, the Commonwealth Secretariat; and Ahmed Ali, Research Officer in the Economic Policy Division, the Commonwealth Secretariat.

Roberts, JP and A Ali, (2016), *The Blue Economy and Small States*. Commonwealth Blue Economy Series, No. 1. Commonwealth Secretariat, London.

Wherever possible, the Commonwealth Secretariat uses paper sourced from sustainable forests or from sources that minimise a destructive impact on the environment.

Copies of this publication may be obtained from

Publications Section
Commonwealth Secretariat
Marlborough House
Pall Mall
London SW1Y 5HX
United Kingdom
Tel: +44 (0)20 7747 6500
Email: publications@commonwealth.int
Web: www.thecommonwealth.org/publications

A catalogue record for this publication is available from the British Library.

ISBN (paperback): 978-1-84929-156-9
ISBN (downloadable e-book): 978-1-84859-950-5

Foreword

The Commonwealth has 2.2 billion citizens, many of whose livelihoods and food security depend upon the world's oceans, seas and coastal areas – the largest ecosystem on the planet. In the years following the 2012 Rio Summit, we have witnessed a marked increase in international awareness of the oceans' potential as a key driver of sustainable economic growth. This contribution was subsequently ratified by the international community's adoption of the Sustainable Development Goals in September 2015. Goal 14 specifically recognises the critical contribution the ocean can make to the development of the smallest and most vulnerable nations. Furthermore, the emergence of the 'blue economy' concept demonstrates a set of practical strategies to ensure that economic activities do not compromise the long-term capacity of ocean ecosystems to support those activities, and remain resilient and healthy.

Managing the oceans effectively is a uniquely cross-national, cross-sectoral challenge. With its cross-cutting nature, the blue economy concept offers a unique opportunity to address complex and inter-connected challenges, without compromising economic growth. This is a concept that, if implemented effectively, can contribute to a significantly broad range of sustainable development outcomes. It has the potential to help countries to make the transition from their current trajectories of over consumption to more resource-efficient societies that rely more strongly on renewable marine resources to satisfy consumers' needs and industry demand, and to tackle climate change.

The Commonwealth has a long history of engagement on issues relating to ocean management and sustainability and, for a number of years, has advocated and promoted the blue economy concept as a holistic means of addressing sustainable development at multiple levels. Indeed, long before the Rio Summit in 2012, Commonwealth Heads of Government had stressed the need for practical outcomes on the blue economy to ensure the sustainable management of oceans as the basis for livelihoods, food security and economic development. Furthermore, most recently, at their meeting in Malta in November 2015, Commonwealth Heads of Government fully acknowledged that the development of a sustainably managed blue economy would offer significant opportunities for economic growth and general development for many Commonwealth states.

In order to fully realise the many opportunities presented by pursuing a blue economy approach, fundamental changes are required to address the matter of ocean governance at the national, regional and global levels. If we are going to create ocean solutions that are sustainable over the long term, we need to recognise the interdependencies of the three dimensions of sustainable development, which must be mutually reinforcing. Fundamentally, existing sectors must be managed in a much more sustainable manner. Small and developing states must also embrace the development of new sectors, many of which have a strong technology base, to achieve more diversified and resilient economies.

Such change can only be realised through strong leadership. Nowhere is this truer than for the ocean, a resource perceived to be everyone's right but no one's responsibility. Creating the political will to implement all elements of a blue economy strategy is a key theme in the assistance and advice the Commonwealth provides to countries. It is our belief that much of the focus and emphasis must be placed on governance in order to successfully transition to a vibrant blue economy. The Commonwealth has a niche and is a global leader in supporting countries to effect the necessary changes.

This *Commonwealth Blue Economy Series* presents a synthesis of information and practical advice to Commonwealth governments relating to the potential deployment of a range of policy options for different sectors and opportunities for the road ahead. In so doing, this series aims to support the development of the blue economy in Commonwealth countries by providing a high-level assessment of the opportunities available for economic diversification and sustainable growth.

Deodat Maharaj
Deputy Secretary-General
Economic and Social Development

Contents

Acronyms and abbreviations

EEZs	exclusive economic zones
EIU	Economist Intelligence Unit
ESCAP	UN Economic and Social Commission for Asia and the Pacific
GDP	gross domestic product
NGOs	non-governmental organisations
NOEP	US National Ocean Economic Program
OECD	Organisation for Economic Co-operation and Development
SDGs	Sustainable Development Goals
SIDS	small island developing states
SMEs	small and micro enterprises
SOPAC	South Pacific Applied Geoscience Commossion
UNCED	United Nations Conference on Environment and Development
UNCTAD	UN Conference on Trade and Development
UNDP	UN Development Programme
UNEP	UN Environment Programme
WWF	World Wide Fund for Nature

Summary

The ocean is an essential part of the world economy – from the uses made of ocean space, the social and economic values we attach to it, the important goods and services it supplies, to the activities it supports. Many small island developing states have jurisdiction over globally significant ocean areas, which typically far exceed their terrestrial footprint and are therefore dependent to a large extent on ocean resources and the sectors they support. Coastal and island nations, both large and small, are increasingly looking to their marine waters to bolster slowing growth in their terrestrial economies by exploring new opportunities for investment and employment.

This fundamental contribution of the ocean reaffirms a critical need to achieve better coherence across the social, economic and environmental pillars of sustainable development, but in a fundamentally different way from the manner in which modern society has historically viewed the balances and linkages up to now. A paradigm shift is needed in how we use and manage ocean resources to reverse current piecemeal approaches that lead to over-exploitation, marine ecosystem degradation and incompatibility of uses. Such a paradigm should be strategic, integrated and cross-sectoral: it must be able to encompass the need for healthy, productive and biologically diverse oceans, well-established and newly emerging economic activities, sustainable livelihoods and secure human settlements.

Since 2012, many small island developing states have embraced the emerging concept of the 'blue economy' as a mechanism for realising sustainable growth centred on an ocean-based economy. In that time, the blue economy has emerged as a key component of a new global dialogue about the role of coastal and ocean waters in sustainable development. For small states, in particular, the concept of the blue economy presents itself as a promising avenue for economic diversification and growth embedded in fundamental principles of environmental sustainability.

A blue economy-centred development approach, which sustainably utilises ocean resources, has the potential to mitigate some of the inherent structural challenges of small states. These include small, undiversified economies, limited fiscal space and the high unit costs of providing public services. These challenges are partly the result of having small populations, small domestic markets and limited conventional natural resources. Some of these countries are also highly vulnerable to extreme weather patterns and climate change, with many only a few metres above sea level and facing natural hazards. Countries that fully implement the blue economy concept have the twin potential of realising economic development benefits that address economic structural challenges, while at the same time improving environmental sustainability.

While there are currently a number of models describing the 'blue' and 'green' economies, there is a critical gap in understanding the full potential of the evolving blue economy concept, particularly in the context of small states. To address this gap, the Commonwealth has launched this *Blue Economy Series* as a means of providing governments with practical advice concerning the implementation of blue economy development frameworks at the national level.

Chapter 1

Oceans and the Global Economy

Chapter 1
Oceans and the Global Economy

The idea of using the sea for economic gain is hardly new. Island nations, in particular, have benefitted from their ocean resources for centuries, with marine uses and activities contributing significantly to their development and overall economies. These include a wide range of maritime sectors essential to both current and future economic development, including: capture fisheries; maritime transport and ports; coastal tourism; mineral exploitation; as well as the marine ecosystems and resources that support them. What clearly is new, however, is a growing appreciation of the critical role the oceans play in sustainable economic growth and, as a corollary, a growing appreciation of the need to better manage and protect coastal and marine ecosystems and resources that are the fundamental basis for that growth.

According to a recent study by the Organisation for Economic Co-operation and Development (OECD 2016), the value of the global ocean economy may be in the order of US$1.5 trillion per annum, contributing approximately 2–3 per cent to the world's gross domestic product (GDP). Marine services, such as tourism and shipping, provide the largest proportion (US$880 billion [bn]), followed by sectors categorised under marine resources (US$377 bn) and marine manufacturing (US$107 bn) (Government of Ireland 2012). Globally, approximately 350 million jobs are linked to the oceans through fishing, aquaculture, coastal and marine tourism and research activities. Moreover, in excess of one billion people depend on fish as their primary source of protein (OECD 2012) (see Figure 1.1).

Research conducted by countries around the world suggests that the ocean economy or ocean industries can produce from 1 to 5 per cent of national GDP (Park and Kildow 2014). For example, in 2014, the US National Ocean Economic Program (NOEP) estimated values for the ocean economy. By its estimates, in 2010, the ocean economy comprised more than 2.7 million jobs and contributed over $258 billion (1.8 per cent) to the GDP of the United States. In the case of China, it is estimated that the ocean economy contributed US$962 bn (10 per cent of GDP) in 2014, employing 9 million people; while in the case of

Figure 1.1 Contribution of the ocean to global economic development

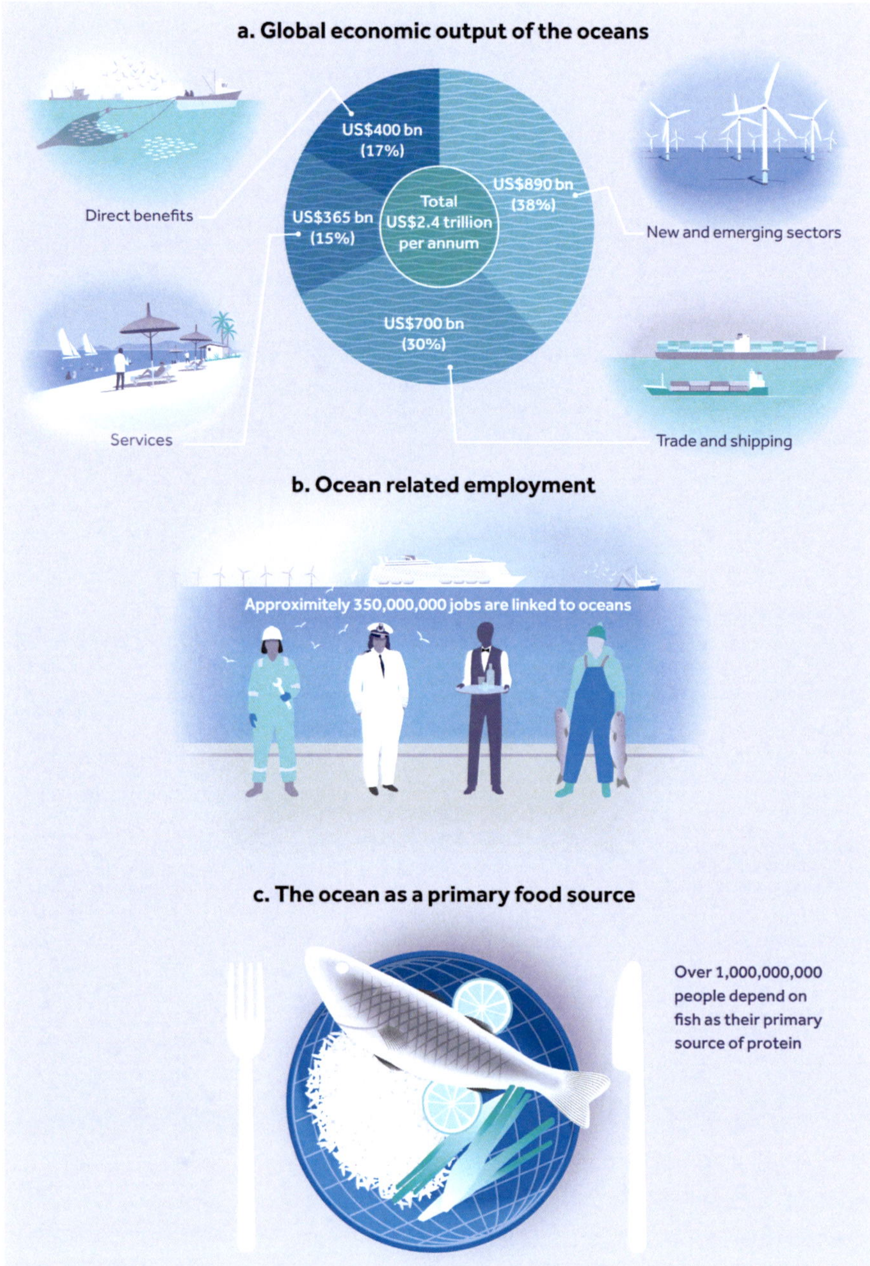

Source: Author's calculation and WWF 2015b

Indonesia, the ocean economy contributed 20 per cent of GDP, comparable with other low middle-income countries with large ocean territories (Economist Intelligence Unit [EIU] 2015).

As well as the direct economic contributions, the ocean also provides a broader range of essential services to human communities that support economic well-being and human health. For example, a recent study by the World Bank and the Commonwealth Secretariat (Hampton and Jeyacheya 2013) estimated that the economic value of coral reef-related tourism and recreation in Indian Ocean small island developing states (SIDS) was in the order of US$1.4 billion, a value that is only surpassed by the coastal protection value of coral reefs (US$1.58 billion).

Recognising this potential, coastal and island nations, both large and small, are looking to their marine waters to bolster slowing growth in their terrestrial economies, discover new opportunities for investment and employment, and build competitive advantage in emerging industries such as deep seabed mining and marine biotechnology. In this context, the emerging concept of the blue economy has gained a great deal of prominence since 2012 as a mechanism for realising sustainable growth centred on an ocean-based economy (Anon, 2014). In that time, the blue economy has emerged as a key component of a new global dialogue about the role of coastal and ocean waters in sustainable development. For small states, in particular, the concept of the blue economy presents itself as a promising avenue for economic diversification and growth embedded in the fundamental principles of environmental sustainability.

1.1 Purpose of this series and summary of volumes

The blue economy has clearly been embraced by many SIDS but, while there currently exist a number of models describing the green and/or blue economies, the critical gap in these concepts, particularly in the context of SIDS, is a mechanism for their implementation. Little, if any, practical information is available to countries wishing to implement these concepts at the national level.

There is, therefore, a need to move beyond the current dialogue on the subject of achieving sustainable development to deliver practical solutions to countries that are pragmatic, realistic and achievable, while at the same time delivering tangible benefits to countries in terms of economic diversification, and food and energy security.

This *Commonwealth Blue Economy Series* aims to support the development of the blue economy in Commonwealth member countries by providing a high-level assessment of some of the opportunities available for economic diversification and sustainable growth in SIDS. To complement this introductory volume, four additional volumes have been prepared. Additional volumes will be added to the series as new information and experience becomes available.

This first volume of the *Commonwealth Blue Economy Series* provides an overview of the opportunities, challenges, barriers, gaps and opportunities in building a blue economy, with a particular focus on SIDS. It is clear that the development of a blue economy in individual countries will face significant challenges and constraints. It is equally clear that the prospects for developing a blue economy and transforming the nascent conceptual framework that has developed over an extended period, are real and capable of achievement. Doing so will require addressing a number of significant gaps and barriers, and addressing a number of both thematic and sectoral enablers.

The countries that succeed in this challenge are likely to be those who are willing to pursue a dual strategy of both investing in improving the management of existing sectors and also in the development of new sectors, for which limited experience or capacity may currently exist.

- **Volume 2** explores the potential for the development of a blue economy aquaculture industry.
- **Volume 3** explores the potential for the further development of capture fisheries as a key contributing sector to the blue economy.
- **Volume 4** explores the potential for and actions needed to progress the generation of energy from marine renewable sources in SIDS.
- **Volume 5** explores the opportunities available for the development of a blue biotechnology sector in SIDS.

Drawing on international experience in the respective sectors, each of these volumes provides recommendations that will assist governments in moving the relevant sector towards becoming an economic reality where opportunities exist. It is hoped that the material presented in this series will stimulate thinking about how SIDS can benefit from the development of the blue economy by integrating different sectors into the 'blue growth' agenda.

References

Anon (2014), 'Blue Economy Concept Paper', available at: https://sustainabledevelopment.un.org/content/documents/2978BEconcept.pdf (accessed 8 April 2016).

Economist Intelligence Unit (EIU) (2015), 'The Blue Economy: Growth, Opportunity and a Sustainable Ocean Economy', an Economist Intelligence Unit briefing paper for the World Ocean Summit 2015, available at: http://www.economistinsights.com/sites/default/files/Blue%20Economy_briefing%20paper_WOS2015.pdf (accessed on 21 March 2016).

Government of Ireland (2012), *Harnessing our Ocean Wealth: An Integrated Marine Plan for Ireland*, Government of Ireland, July 2012, 8, available at: http://www.ouroceanwealth.ie/SiteCollectionDocuments/Harnessing%20Our%20Ocean%20Wealth%20Report.pdf (accessed 7 April 2016).

Hampton, MP and J Jeyacheya (2013), *Tourism and Inclusive Growth in Small Island Developing States*, Commonwealth Secretariat, London.

Millennium Ecosystem Assessment (2005), *Ecosystems and Human Well-being: Biodiversity Synthesis*, World Resources Institute Washington, DC, available at: http://www.millenniumassessment.org/documents/document.356.aspx.pdf (accessed 1 April 2016).

Organisation for Economic Co-operation and Development (OECD) (2016), *The Ocean Economy in 2030*, OECD Publishing, Paris.

OECD (2012), The Future of the Ocean Economy: Exploring the prospects for emerging ocean industries to 2030, draft OECD Project Proposal Document, 15, available at: http://www.oecd.org/futures/Future%20of%20the%20Ocean%20Economy%20Project%20Proposal.pdf (accessed 7 April 2016).

Park, KS and JT Kildow (2014), 'A study on rebuilding the classification system of the ocean economy', *Journal of Ocean and Coastal Economics* Vol. 2014, Article 4, 37, available at: http://cbe.miis.edu/cgi/viewcontent.cgi?article=1001&context=joce (accessed 22 March 2016).

Chapter 2

The Blue Economy Concept

Chapter 2
The Blue Economy Concept

2.1 Defining the blue economy

The 'blue economy' concept was first coined during the 2012 United Nations Conference on Sustainable Development (Silver et al. 2015), (hereafter the '2012 Rio Summit'). It is an evolving concept that recognises the need to maximise the enormous economic potential presented by the ocean, while preserving it.

Derived from the 'green economy' concept endorsed at the same meeting, the blue economy shares the same desired outcome: the improvement of human well-being and social equity, while significantly reducing environmental risks and ecological scarcities (UN Conference on Trade and Development [UNCTAD] 2014). However, unlike the conventional development model, where financial and physical capital are seen to be given priority over human and natural capital, the green economy deliberately seeks to invest more in social and environmental outcomes (UN Economic and Social Commission for Asia and the Pacific [ESCAP] 2012). This new approach aims to scale up traditional uses of the ocean, using the latest technologies and steered by new, enabling public policies (World Wide Fund for Nature [WWF] 2015).

A recent UN Environment Programme (UNEP) study into the benefits of transitioning to a green economy (UNEP 2011) highlighted three broad conclusions that are highly relevant to the blue economy: (i) in a transition to a green economy, new jobs are created, which over time exceed the losses in 'brown economy' jobs; (ii) transitioning to a green economy not only increases wealth over the long term, but also produces a higher rate of GDP growth; and (iii) there is a clear link between poverty eradication and better protection and restoration of habitats, marine fisheries resources and biodiversity.

The specific concept of the blue economy stems from the realisation that, with the extensive marine areas with which many SIDS are endowed, the future resource base for such countries is predominantly marine. Since a large portion of marine resources is believed to have remained untapped or unexplored in different marine zones of the world, there is a widespread conviction that the future source of growth is probably contingent upon the efficient utilisation of those rich ocean resources. This significant per capita marine resource base means, therefore, that the blue economy offers the prospect of sustained, environmentally sound, socially inclusive economic [blue] growth. As noted by Mohanty et al. (2015), '*its importance is realised prominently after the unprecedented contraction of global output and employment affecting the livelihoods of millions of people in different regions of the world*'.

With sustainable growth the new focus of the global policy discourse, countries seeking to develop their ocean economies have, to varying degrees, acknowledged the need for policies that better align future economic growth in their seas with maintaining or even restoring ocean health. However, while the idea of the blue economy or 'blue growth' has become synonymous with the 'greening' of the ocean economy (Onguglo and Eugui 2014), and the frame by which governments, non-governmental organisations (NGOs) and others refer to a more sustainable ocean economy, these emerging concepts remain ill-defined and open to wide, and often different, interpretations (Silver et al. 2015).

One general interpretation of the blue economy is that it can maximise the economic value of the marine environment in a sustainable manner that preserves and protects the sea's resources and ecosystems. By that definition, the blue economy can be broadly defined to include 'economic activity which directly or indirectly uses the sea as an input' (Morrissey et al. 2010).

2.1.1 The blue economy and the emerging sustainable development agenda

While the contemporary concept of the blue economy may be relatively new, the sustainable utilisation of the oceans as the basis for sustainable development is certainly not a new concept. The 1992 United Nations Conference on Environment and Development (UNCED) in Rio de Janeiro, and thereafter the subsequent 10th and 20th anniversary World Summits, reaffirmed the essential role of the ocean across the social, economic and environmental pillars of sustainable development. It was encapsulated comprehensively in chapter 17 of Agenda 21, adopted at UNCED, which is devoted to the protection of the ocean, seas and coastal areas, as well as the protection, rational use and development of their living resources, and reiterated in numerous action plans, resolutions and statements.

More recently, the post-2015 development agenda, adopted by the UN General Assembly in September 2015,[1] includes a broad framework which reflects the multifaceted nature of development, including: (a) environmental sustainability, productive employment and decent work, and equality; (b) the enablers of development or strategies; (c) strengthened consultations at the conception stage to build ownership and to avoid the perception of a donor-centric agenda; and (d) institutional building and structural transformations.

Of particular importance to the discussion on the blue economy are the Sustainable Development Goals (SDGs), adopted as part of the post-2015 agenda. They include, in Goal 14 (see Figure 2.1),

Figure 2.1 Sustainable development goal 14

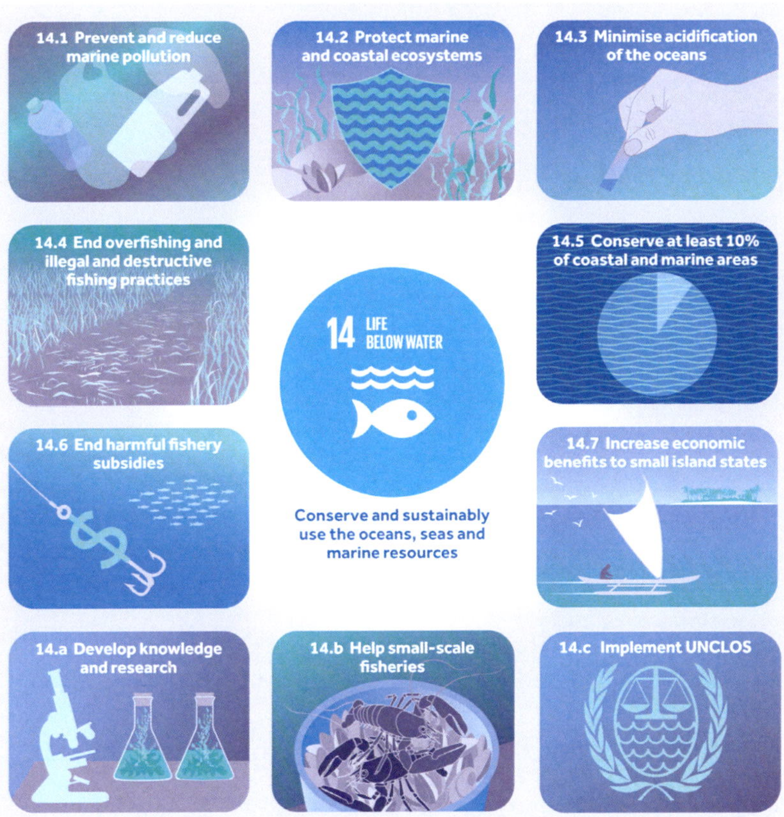

a specific reference that articulates the link between oceans and sustainable development in a way that has previously not been explicitly stated. Goal 14 places the oceans more centrally on the development agenda, thereby creating new opportunities to focus the efforts of the development and donor community on this essential aspect of sustainable development; it also provides a basis for measuring progress (see Boxe 2.1).

The Abu Dhabi Declaration adopted by the High-Level Event on the Blue Economy in January 2014 stressed the contribution that an oceans economy can make towards the alleviation of hunger, poverty eradication, creation of sustainable livelihoods and mitigation of climate change. There is, therefore, a clear recognition that the concepts and objectives of sustainable

Box 2.1 The blue economy and the sustainable development goals

- Effective implementation of Goal 14 would undoubtedly contribute to improved management of fishery resources, which in turn would contribute to achieving Goal 2 relating to food security.
- Coastal ecosystems, such as mangroves and coral reefs, can play a significant role in mitigating the impacts of climate-related phenomena. Therefore, a focus on coastal habitat protection would contribute directly to Goal 13, which relates to resilience and adaptive capacities to climate-related hazards.
- Using ocean-based renewable energy sources to reduce reliance on imported petroleum-based fuels in SIDS would contribute directly to Goal 7, which relates to sustainable energy, as well as contributing to the state's climate change policies, which link to Goal 13.
- The amount of by-catch and fishery waste that is not utilised is a major source of inefficiency in fisheries. Achieving this outcome would contribute to Goal 12, which relates to sustainable consumption patterns.
- The blue economy has the potential to contribute significantly to sustainable economic growth and higher-quality employment (Goal 8). The development of new sectors, such as aquaculture, could contribute to addressing such fundamental issues as food security, development of small and micro enterprises (SMEs), diversifying economies and reducing pressure on capture fisheries, to name but a few.
- Implementation of the blue economy must be supported by human capacity development, investment in new technologies, and ongoing research to improve knowledge and facilitate more informed decision-making. These are some of the fundamental principles included in Goal 17, which relates to the implementation of sustainable development.

development and the green economy make sense only if the ocean is fully incorporated into development planning. As noted by Onguglo and Eugui (2014), '*it seeks to expand economic, production and trade activities beyond land territories to oceans-based marine environment, related biodiversity, ecosystem, species and genetic resources, while preserving and ensuring their sustainable use and management under national jurisdictional and international oceans and seas including marine living organisms (from fish and algae to micro-organisms) and natural resources in the seabed*'.

In this regard, notwithstanding the importance of SDG 14, it should be recognised that the blue economy maps across several of the SDGs. It is not a simple relationship between the blue economy and SDG 14, but a complex inter-relationship that highlights how an effective blue economy framework, supported by the protection and sustainable utilisation of marine ecosystem services, can contribute to multiple outcomes reflected through the SDGs as a whole (see Boxe 2.2).

Over time, it is argued, the SDGs can help mobilise significant additional financial, technical and institutional resources, while focusing on specific targets will help attract new partnerships, new technologies and institutional, human and financial resources (Rustomjee 2016).

2.2 Priorities for the blue economy

While no universally agreed definition exists for the blue economy, it is possible to describe what the blue economy may

Box 2.2 Marine ecosystems services

This link between nature and the economy is often described using the concept of ecosystem services, or the flows of values to human societies as a result of the state and quality of 'natural capital'. The Millennium Ecosystem Assessment (2005) provides a useful four-category framework within which to view ecosystem services that contribute to human well-being, each underpinned by biodiversity:

The concept of ecosystem services provides a framework to recognise the many benefits of nature – by maintaining stocks of this natural capital we can allow the sustained provision of flows of ecosystem services, and thereby ensure future human well-being. Some, such as provisioning services can be valued in financial terms, while other non-use values are often influential in decision-making, but are rarely valued in monetary terms.

look like by the prominence of certain characteristics. A review of approaches to the green economy highlights seven strongly inter-linked characteristics that should be prominent in an effective blue economy framework:

1. It recognises the essential value of natural capital as the basis for a healthy marine environment which supports the ongoing supply of marine goods and services;
2. It maintains growth, fosters 'blue' business and promotes jobs in 'blue' sectors;
3. It promotes energy from low-carbon and renewable sources;
4. It addresses resource scarcity and promotes enhanced resource efficiency through improved and enhanced natural resource management;
5. It ensures resilience from foreseeable impacts of climate change through developing adaptive capacities;
6. It supports the building of the technical capacity needed to achieve the government's stated goals; and
7. It promotes sustainable management of our ecosystem and finite resources.

The scope of the blue economy can vary depending on the sectors considered. Economic sectors using oceans and inland waters include fisheries, aquaculture, tourism, shipping, biotechnologies, maritime security, mining, oil and gas, and renewable energy. These various sectors have a direct impact on the aquatic ecosystems, and the fauna and flora they sustain. The aim of an overarching blue economy framework should therefore be to assess ways and means to mitigate the cumulative impact of these economic sectors on the living marine resources and ecosystem services. In numerous coastal developing countries, including several SIDS, blue economy frameworks have been adopted to promote at the initial stages food security and decent livelihoods. Such approaches generally include fisheries, aquaculture, ecosystem services, and marine and coastal tourism, with the potential for future integration of other important sectors as appropriate (Ababouch 2015).

The challenge is where to start in order to alter course to achieve a blue economy, and in so doing to develop or strengthen social, economic and environmental linkages and reform current governance arrangements. This will require some fundamental

Box 2.3 The importance of value chains

Many of the economic activities listed in Table 2.1 will be surrounded by both upstream and downstream activities (the value chain) (Figure 2.2):

It is important to consider these value chains in the context of the blue economy, since large parts of the economic activities take place not in core sectors themselves, but in adjacent economic activities. For example, think of maritime transport where the actual shipping is the visualisation of the economic activity, but large parts of the added value are created in seaports and services associated to this, as well as in the shipyards and other supply industry activities required for shipping. Similarly, for capture fisheries, opportunities exist to extend the value chain with both upstream activities (e.g. vessel support services) and downstream activities (e.g. processing whole fish into higher-value products). The extent to which the value chain can be extended will ultimately determine the total value that can be realised from a single maritime function or resource.

Value chains can also be seen as a vehicle through which new forms of production, technologies, logistics, labour processes and organisational relations and networks are introduced. The value chain therefore acts as a value multiplier, which can significantly increase the overall value of the blue economy without significantly increasing pressure on natural resources.

changes in the way the ocean is managed at the national, regional and global scales to create a more harmonised and integrated approach.

While it is clearly recognised that the ocean offers further potential for economic benefits to be derived from the

Table 2.1 Established and emerging ocean-based activities

Established	Emerging
Capture fisheries	Marine aquaculture
Seafood processing	Deep- and ultra-deep water oil and gas
Shipping	Offshore wind energy
Ports	Ocean renewable energy
Shipbuilding and repair	Marine and seabed mining
Offshore oil and gas (shallow water)	Maritime safety and surveillance
Marine manufacturing and construction	Marine biotechnology
Maritime and coastal tourism	High-tech marine products and services
Marine business services	Others
Marine R&D and education	
Dredging	

Source: OECD 2016

Figure 2.2 Capture fishery value chains

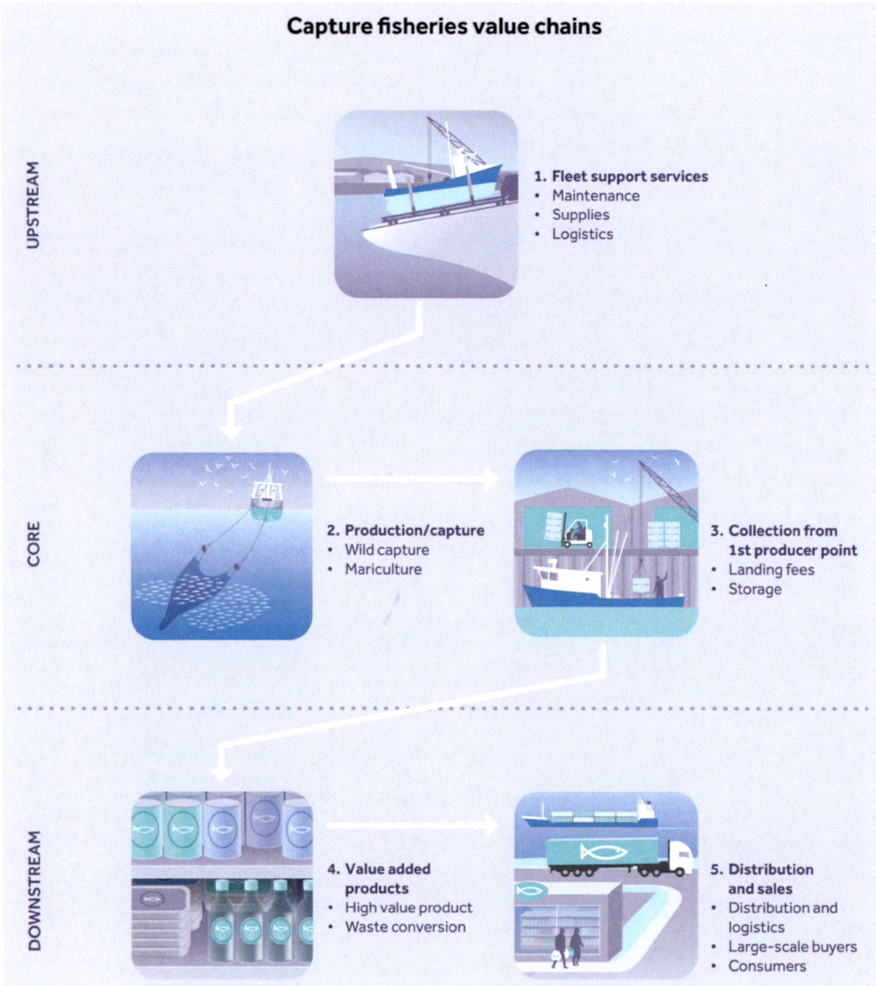

sea – both from living and non-living resources – it is not always clear what a sustainable ocean economy should look like, and under what conditions it is most likely to develop (EIU 2015). In order to achieve this, two areas of focus are necessary:

1. Improve and optimise the economic returns from existing activities and resource utilisation; and
2. Explore opportunities for the development of new economic sectors.

2.3 Optimising returns from existing activities

The list of sectors relevant to the blue economy is very wide (Table 2.1) and the potential of the oceans is manifold and complex.

The potential exists to more effectively exploit many of the existing resources and to optimise returns from existing activities. Opportunities to further develop and utilise existing sectors as a means to create jobs and to increase the value of those sectors therefore need to be assessed in the context of the blue economy. In the specific case of SIDS, this will most likely relate primarily to coastal and marine tourism and capture fisheries.

In terms of future uses of the oceans, a number of new and emerging opportunities have been identified that can contribute to the development of the blue economy. Among these emerging opportunities having particularly strong potential in small states are fish farming (aquaculture), ocean-based renewable energy, ocean-related tourism and marine biotechnology. We discuss these in more detail in the following chapter.

Endnote

1 Further information about the post-2015 development agenda is available at: https://sustainabledevelopment.un.org/sdgs (accessed 8 April 2016).

References

Ababouch, L (2015), *Fisheries and Aquaculture in the Context of Blue Economy*, UN Economic Commission for Africa, Senegal.

Economist Intelligence Unit (EIU) (2015), 'The Blue Economy: Growth, Opportunity and a Sustainable Ocean Economy', an Economist Intelligence Unit briefing paper for the World Ocean Summit 2015, available at: http://www.economistinsights.com/sites/default/files/Blue%20Economy_briefing%20paper_WOS2015.pdf (accessed on 21 March 2016).

Economic and Social Commission for Asia and the Pacific (ESCAP) (2012), *Green Economy in a Blue World: Pacific Perspectives*, United Nations Economic and Social Commission for Asia and the Pacific, Suva, Fiji.

Mohanty, SK, P Dash, A Gupta and P Gaur (2015), *Prospects of Blue Economy in the Indian Ocean*, RIS, New Delhi.

Morrissey, K, S Hynes, M Cuddy and C O'Donoghue (2010), *Ireland's Ocean Economy*, report prepared by the Socio-Economic Marine Research Unit (SEMRU), JE Cairnes School of Business and Economics, National University of Ireland, Galway.

Organisation for Economic Co-operation and Development (OECD) (2016), *The Ocean Economy in 2030*, OECD Publishing, Paris.

Onguglo, B and DV Eugui (2014), 'The Oceans Economy for Small Island Developing States', *Commonwealth Hot Trade Topics* Issue 110, Commonwealth Secretariat, London.

Rustomjee, C (2016), 'Developing the Blue Economy in Caribbean and Other Small States', CIGI Policy Brief No. 75, Centre for International Governance Innovation, Ontario.

Silver, JJ, NJ Gray, LM Campbell, LW Fairbanks and RL Gruby (2015), 'Blue economy and competing discourses in international oceans governance', *Journal of Environment & Development*, Vol 24,135–106.

UNCTAD (2015), *Review of Maritime Transport*, UNCTAD, Geneva.

UNCTAD (2014), *The Oceans Economy: Opportunities and Challenges for Small Island Developing States*, UNCTAD, Geneva.

UN Environment Programme (UNEP) (2011), *Towards a Green Economy: Pathways to Sustainable Development and Poverty Eradication*, UNEP, Nairobi.

World Wide Fund for Nature (WWF) (2015), *All Hands on Deck: Setting Course Towards a Sustainable Blue Economy*, WWF Baltic Ecoregion Programme, available at: http://wwf.panda.org/wwf_news/?254101/All-Hands-on-Deck-Setting-Course-to-a-Sustainable-Blue-Economy-in-the-Baltic-Sea-Region (accessed 22 March 2016).

Chapter 3

The Blue Economy and Small States

Chapter 3
The Blue Economy and Small States

3.1 The blue economy potential in small states

Small states are primarily located in the Caribbean, Pacific and Indian Ocean regions, and face distinctive challenges, some of which are inherent in their small size and geographical location. The economic costs to being small manifest themselves in a number of ways, including small domestic markets and limited export volume. Small size also restricts the number of activities these states can engage in, blunting economic diversification and returns to scale in both the public and private sectors (Easterly and Kraay 2000; Briguglio 2014). They also have a high unit cost for the provision of public services, including policy formulation, data collection and regulatory activities, all of which are key for developing an ocean economy. In addition, their small populations limit the potential pool of qualified civil servants, which are typically stretched handling large portfolios.

The location of small states also presents a number of challenges. Many are isolated from major markets and trading hubs, increasing transportation, freight and communications costs (UN Development Programme [UNDP] 2014). They are highly vulnerable to climate change – it is an existential threat in some countries – with many countries only a few metres above sea level and facing natural hazards, including extreme weather events that can sometimes set back development by a generation. Small states also face a challenging development finance context. Some of these challenges were highlighted in the Addis Ababa Action Agenda document, but they continue to face many hurdles, including limited domestic resources, low tax potential, low savings rates, limited tax capacity and high debt ratios.[1] These challenges – size, low economies of scale, climate change, remoteness, and limited funding and natural resources – constrain the capacity of small states to realise sustainable development.

Oceans and their vast economic resources present new avenues for realising sustainable economic development in small states. Typically in these countries, the extent of their maritime space, including their extensive exclusive economic zones (EEZs) constitute a larger geographic area than their land territory. For example, the EEZ of The Bahamas is estimated to be 242,970 square miles compared to its land area of 5,383 square miles, whereas St Vincent and the Grenadines' is estimated to be about 13,900 square miles, more than 90 times its land area. In the case of St Kitts and Nevis, the ocean space is almost 7,900 square miles, while the state has a land area of only 100 square miles.

The blue economy concept is centred on the sustainable utilisation of ocean resources, and with support from the Commonwealth Secretariat many countries are now assessing the potential economic value or their oceanic waters. However, for this to be an affective development policy, it should factor in the unique structural challenges of small states and better contextualise recommendations. Partly the reason why the blue economy has garnered significant attention in recent years is its potential to overcome some of these structural challenges and realise sustainable development at multiple levels. The concept is still evolving, but the key sectors for small states include fishing, maritime transport and tourism. We now review recent developments in these sectors, challenges and their growth potential, and contribution to sustainable development in the future.

3.2 Fishing

Fish and fish products are an important subset of the blue economy in most small states. Fish is a key source of nutrition, employment and export receipts in many small states and is essential for the economic survival of many small states. Total global exports of fish and fishing products in 2015 was estimated at just under US$143 billion, an 8 per cent increase from the previous year. Exports from SIDS dropped slightly in 2014 to US$1.7 billion and, as shown in Figure 3.1, the drop has been slightly steeper in Commonwealth small states.[2] As a percentage of total exports, SIDS contribute just over 1 per cent to world production of fish and fish products. However, fisheries account for 3 per cent of GDP in SIDS, but for some small states this figure can increase to more than 10 per cent (UNCTAD 2016).

There is a regional variation between countries, with four of the top five exporting Commonwealth small states[3] from Africa – Namibia, Mauritius, Seychelles and Maldives – while the bottom five are from the Caribbean (see Figure 3.2). Export revenues

Figure 3.1 Total export of fish and fish products US$ billions

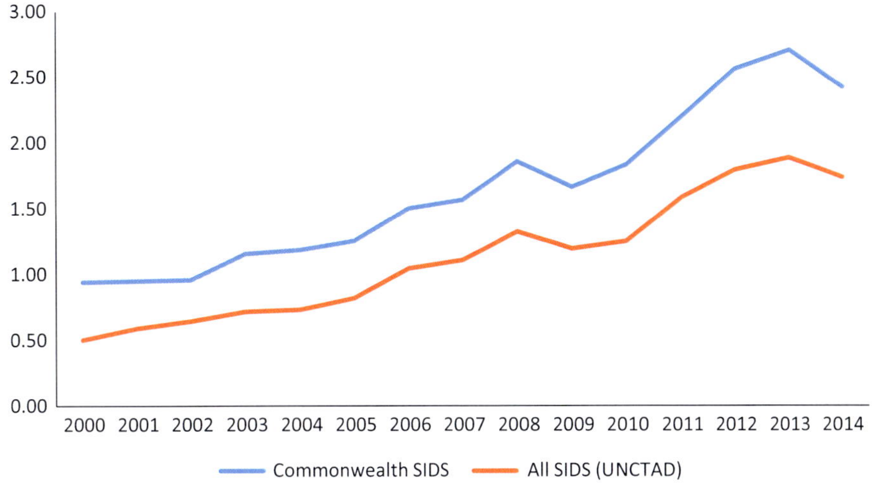

Source: UNCTAD 2016

from fish products has been steadily increasing for the top five commonwealth small states but plateaued after 2012, while in contrast exports from countries in the lower end have been characterised by sharp fluctuations in exports (UNCTAD 2016).

Going forward, the importance of fish and fish products to small states – both as a source of protein and contribution to GDP – is likely to continue. However, based on their assessed capacity and increasing global demand for fish products, small states have the potential to further develop and grow this subsector of

Figure 3.2 The ocean economy in Mauritius

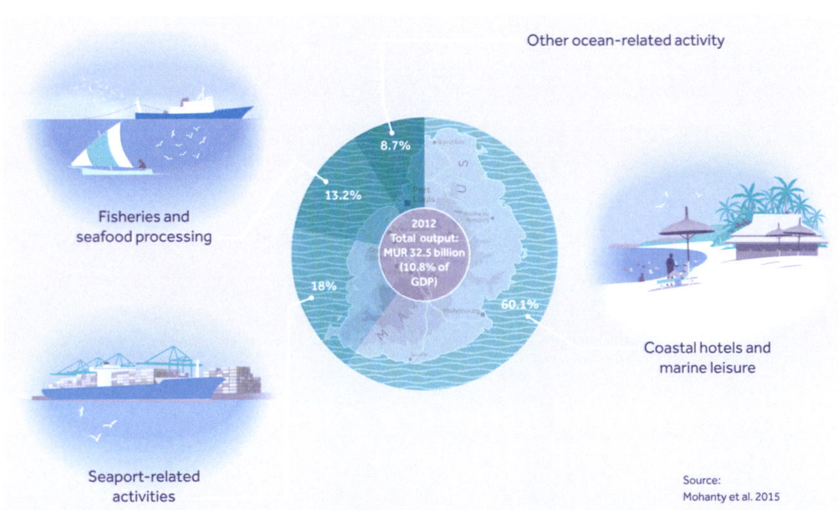

the blue economy. For example, fish and fish products exports from Pacific SIDS has the potential to contribute between 30 and 80 per cent to GDP given the potential economic value of their large EEZs (Ababouch 2015). Fully realising this, however, will require an enabling policy and regulatory environment that ensures domestic firms participate in sustainable harvesting of local and regional fish stocks (UNCTAD 2014).

3.3 Maritime transport

More than 50 per cent of the global population, large cities and key industrial hubs are concentrated in coastal areas. Close proximity to coasts enables easy access to international markets – over 90 per cent of global trade is seaborne; continuous inflows and outflows of products and resources; and easy transport links for goods and people.

Global seaborne shipments increased by 3.2 per cent in 2014 to more than 9.84 billion tons from the previous year, and are forecasted to continue growing at a moderate pace in 2015/16 (UNCTAD 2016). Maritime transport plays an important role in the economies of small states given their reliance on imports and openness to international trade. It is difficult to attain disaggregated data on the full role of these countries, but a disproportionally high number of ships from third countries have registered their vessels in these countries. Open registries can increase government revenues of hosting countries, and reduce red tape and costs for ship owners.

As shown in Table 3.1, the registration is led by Caribbean small states, but this is expected given the high number of vessels passing through the Panama Canal (UNCTAD 2016; Roberts 2015). Commonwealth small states have a disproportionately high share of merchant fleets registered in their countries, accounting for above 7 per cent of total fleets since 2011. Importantly, however, there is significant untapped economic potential in upstream value chains in financial and logistical services, which these countries can better leverage. The economic contribution of maritime transport and its potential to drive growth in small states is therefore significant, but remains underexploited.

3.4 Coastal tourism

Tourism is essential to the economic survival of many small states and is a key sector in their national development plans.

Table 3.1 Commonwealth small states' merchant fleets by flag of registration

	2011	2012	2013	2014	2015
The Bahamas	1,407	1,431	1,436	1,422	1,421
Antigua and Barbuda	1,193	1,295	1,280	1,235	1,174
St Vincent and the Grenadines	1,053	1,000	980	990	963
Belize	860	748	758	771	765
Vanuatu	383	430	433	439	442
St Kitts and Nevis	309	257	266	277	299
Tuvalu	212	182	194	207	228
World	83,283	84,709	86,484	87,926	89,464
Commonwealth % of world total	7.7%	7.5%	7.3%	7.2%	7.0%

Global tourist numbers increased by 5 per cent in 2014 to almost 1.2 billion, but arrivals to small states grew at the faster rate of 9 per cent to roughly 19 million. The sector is a key source of hard currency for these countries, and receipts as a percentage of total exports increased from 29 to 34 per cent in 2014. Caribbean small states have recovered from the decline in receipts caused by the 2008 financial crisis and the sector now accounts for 41 per cent of total export revenues (World Bank 2016). Cruise tourism is a fast-growing sector in the region, and accounts for 50 per cent of global market share by vessel calls and passenger count. However, cruise tourism in the region has been characterised by high volumes and low value. In 2013, for example, the value of receipts from the average tourist visiting the Caribbean was US$1,284 compared to US$1,522 for the Pacific Islands (World Bank 2016).

The tourism sector has also recovered from the drop in foreign direct investment, with green-field investments reaching US$475 million in 2012. This is an increase of 44 per cent from 2011, indicating the growth potential of this key subset of the blue economy for small states (UNCTAD 2014). Nonetheless, there is a growing list of challenges to coastal tourism and marine sustainability, not least climate change, extreme weather events and pollution. Rising sea levels is the biggest threat to coastal areas in the long-term, but uncontrolled mass tourism damaging coastal ecosystems is the most pressing. Ethical tourism, which sets ecological and infrastructure standards, is a growing sector and can advance environmental sustainability in small states.

3.5 Potential blue economy growth sectors

3.5.1 Aquaculture

As discussed earlier, small states have the potential to increase capture fish production. However, global demand for fisheries is expected to grow at a faster pace than global capture fisheries production. The surplus in demand can be met by growth in aquaculture, which is projected to expand by a third, reaching almost 80 MT by 2021, most of which will probably occur in the ocean (OECD 2012).

There are, however, many constraints affecting the prospects of aquaculture production. These include limited opportunities for sites for new operations along increasingly crowded, multiple-user coastal areas, as well as a number of environmental challenges – such as the ability of the environment to accommodate increasing discharges of nutrients and pollution, the threat of the introduction of alien invasive species, and damage to key habitats during the development of aquaculture sites.

3.5.2 Ocean-based renewable energy

Small states economies are reliant on fuel imports for generating energy, which leaves them vulnerable to international price fluctuations. Moving to renewable sources of energy is a priority for many of these countries and given recent technological advances, many are reviewing the potential of their oceans to generate energy. Ocean-based energy refers to all sources of energy that are obtained by either harnessing certain characteristics of ocean power (wave, tidal, thermal conversion, salinity gradient) or by utilising ocean space (offshore wind energy). With growing concern over climate change and increasing global interest in renewable energy, investment in ocean-based energy is expected to grow over the next few decades.

Many small states have the potential to produce significant amounts of ocean-based energy, but are limited by physical constraints or lack of investment. In the Caribbean, for example, offshore wind farms have been discussed as a potential energy source given the region's high population density, but steep drop-offs within a relatively short distance from the coast has inhibited their development (Atherley-Ikechi 2016). Floating wind turbines are currently being piloted in Europe and North America, but are only expected to be available in the Caribbean after 2025.[4] In the Pacific, a study conducted in six Pacific island countries showed that wave power generation has the greatest potential of the ocean-based energy resources, but the capacity and financial resources to adopt and sustain energy conversion technologies is presently weak (South Pacific Applied Geoscience Commossion [SOPAC] 2009).

Other ocean-based renewable energy resources are still at a nascent stage, but there are ongoing pilot projects to test their viability in small states. However, the costs and scalability of the technologies pose difficult questions and limit their full potential in the short term. In summary, the long-term potential for ocean power is significant and widespread, though the technologies are at various stages of development.

3.5.3 Biotechnology

'Marine biotechnology' refers to the use of marine living organisms for industrial and other purposes, such as the synthesis of novel chemical compounds or exploitation of pharmacological properties. Biotechnology has the potential to address a raft of major global challenges, such as sustainable food supplies, human health, energy security and environmental remediation, and to make a significant contribution to green growth in many industrial sectors. At the same time, marine bio-resources also provide a number of important ecosystem services for the planet and its inhabitants and these must be maintained. Examples of marine biotechnology include the following:

- On the health front, there has been increasing interest in marine microbes, particularly bacteria, with studies demonstrating that they are a rich source of potential drugs.
- Marine biotechnology has also displayed widespread commercial potential in industrial products and processes, and in the life sciences industry as a novel source of enzymes and polymers.
- On the energy front, algal biofuels appear to offer promising prospects. Within the last two years, billions of dollars have been injected into alga-culture or algal farming right around the world.

Marine genetic resources found within the EEZ of a country are subject to national jurisdictions, including access and benefit sharing (ABS) laws. However, few small states have specific laws dealing with ABS genetic resources, making it difficult for them to regulate bio-prospecting activities and ensure they benefit from any discoveries. This is particularly important for small states, given their likely reliance on international technological and scientific knowhow – and possibly foreign firms – to exploit these resources (UNCTAD 2014). Tightening their legal and regulatory frameworks, and introducing ABS laws, will be key if they are to receive their share of economic benefits and ensure long-term environmental and resource sustainability.

3.5.4 Blue carbon opportunities, climate change mitigation and resilience

Information made available within the last few years shows how the natural carbon capacity and green infrastructure of key ecosystems at the coast can be used to help tackle the increasing problems being encountered from climate change. The revelation to many people that coastal ecosystems such as mangroves and seagrass meadows trap and store vast quantities of carbon has created new interest for exploring the role of these ecosystems in climate change adaptation and mitigation schemes (Commonwealth Secretariat 2013b).

These same ecosystems are already known to provide many other services to humanity, such as protection from coastal erosion and buffering storm surges and tsunamis. So the addition of carbon sinks opens up new opportunities for valuing the services provided by these ecosystems. Recognising the value of natural capital at the coast is now seen as one of the essential elements for coastal and island states in building a successful green economy. Acting to conserve these habitats now is critically important and represents a shift to the blue economy by developing new carbon markets, creating new investment streams and new jobs, and delivering on biodiversity targets.

Approaches that recognise the true 'carbon' value of coastal ecosystems as part of ecosystem-based mitigation also fit well with global best practice emerging for planners and managers on tackling climate change, and display characteristics that suggest effective uptake can result in reforming of often-inadequate existing policy, legislation and decision-making.

Endnotes

1 At the end of 2013, roughly 50 per cent of small states in the Commonwealth had a debt-to-GDP ratio exceeding more than 60 per cent (Robinson 2015).
2 This excludes the advanced Commonwealth countries of Cyprus and Malta.
3 The fifth-top exporting country is Fiji Islands.
4 For a detailed review of the Caribbean energy landscape see Atherley-Ilkechi (2016).

References

Ababouch, L (2015), *Fisheries and Aquaculture in the Context of Blue Economy*, UN Economic Commission for Africa, Senegal.

Atherley-Ikechi, MA (2016), 'Energy: the Key to a Cleaner, More Prosperous Caribbean', in Lewis-Bynoe, D, *Acheiving a Resilient Future for Small States: Caribbean 2050*, Commonwealth Secretariat, London, 91–93.

Briguglio, L (2014), *A Vulnerability and Resilience Framework for Small States*, University of Malta, Malta.

Commonwealth Secretariat (2013b), *The Management of Coastal Carbon Sinks in Vanuatu: Realising the Potential*, Commonwealth Secretariat, London, available at: http://thecommonwealth.org/sites/default/files/project/documents/The%20Management%20of%20Coastal%20Carbon%20Sinks%20in%20Vanuatu%20-%20Realising%20the%20Potential.pdf. (accessed 7 April 2016).

Easterly, W and A Kraay (2000), 'Small States, Small Problems? Income, Growth, and Volatility in Small States', *World Development*, Vol. 28, 2013–2027.

OECD (2012), The Future of the Ocean Economy: Exploring the prospects for emerging ocean industries to 2030, draft OECD Project Proposal Document, 15, available at: http://www.oecd.org/futures/Future%20of%20the%20Ocean%20Economy%20Project%20Proposal.pdf (accessed 7 April 2016).

Roberts, J (2015), 'The Blue Economy: From Concept to Reality in the Caribbean Region', information paper presented at the inaugural Caribbean Region Dialogue with the G20 Development Working Group, Washington, DC, 13 April 2015, available at: https://www.central-bank.org.tt/sites/default/files/Caribbean_Blue_Economy.pdf (accessed 25 April 2016).

Robinson, M (2015), *Assessment of Debt Restructuring Operations in Commonwealth Small States*, Commonwealth Secretariat, London.

Pacific Islands Applied Geoscience Commission (SOPAC) (2009), *SOPAC Desktop Study of Ocean-Based Renewable Energy Technologies*, SOPAC Miscellaneous Report No. 701, SOPAC; Fiji.

UN Conference on Trade and Development (UNCTAD) (2016), UNCTAD Statistics, available at: http://unctad.org/meetings/en/Presentation/ditc-ted-05082015-vanuatu-3-vivas.pdf (accessed 13 April 2016).

UNCTAD (2014), *The Oceans Economy: Opportunities and Challenges for Small Island Developing States*, UNCTAD, Geneva.

UN Development Programme (UNDP) (2014), *Island Innovations – Leveraging the Environment for Sustainable Development of Small Island Developing States*, United Nations Development Programme, New York.

World Bank (2016), *World Development Indicators*, World Bank, available at: http://databank.worldbank.org/data/reports.aspx?source=2&country=&series=ST.INT.ARVL&period=# (accessed 14 April 2016).

Chapter 4

Growing the Blue Economy

Chapter 4
Growing the Blue Economy

4.1 Barriers to blue growth

The blue economy is strongly dependent on a quality environment for the sustained supply of goods and services. This is particularly true in the case of small states. Over the past century, however, human use of the world's ocean areas has increased exponentially, reflecting intensification of historical ocean uses (e.g. fishing and maritime transportation) and the emergence of new uses, such as the extraction of offshore oil and gas deposits, and seabed minerals. At a global level, heightened food insecurity and diminished economic opportunities are just some of the challenges faced by the world's poorest people as a result of the overexploitation and poor management of the oceans (UNCTAD 2014).

The interconnected nature of ocean and coastal environments means that exploitation of one type of marine resource has the capacity to impact on other marine resources and the wider marine environment. These factors present both governments and ocean users with significant challenges in terms of ensuring that development goals, strategies and projects do not operate at cross-purposes with the vast range of human activities affecting the ocean.

Oceans are facing significant existential ecological risks that can negatively affect the social and economic prospects of all countries, particularly SIDS that are acutely dependent on oceans. The range of threats being faced by the oceans is broad, but the most significant include:

- unsustainable fishing practices;
- pollution from land-based and marine activities;
- marine invasive species;
- habitat destruction from coastal development and extractive industries; and
- poor governance practices.

Notwithstanding the significance of these challenges, the greatest systemic threat facing the ocean in many countries is climate change. Among the many challenges arising from climate change, four appear to be particularly relevant constraints to building the blue economy in SIDS:

- First is sea-level rise, which presents the biggest challenge for small island states and leads to island abandonment, exposure to storm surges, and damage to coastal economies and infrastructure. The sea-level rise anticipated from climate change is the biggest long-term threat facing the tourism industry in many SIDS, where most tourism infrastructure lies just above sea level. Port infrastructure is also vulnerable, although to a lesser extent.
- Second, meeting the demand for water in SIDS will be strongly compromised under most climate change scenarios.
- Third, changes in the ocean and coastal marine environment, such as elevated sea surface temperatures and ocean acidification, will disrupt critical ecosystem services, for example coral reefs and fisheries, which small islands depend upon for food and economic development.
- Finally, a further significant impact of climate change is physical damage from hurricanes and other severe weather events. Significant reef damage and alteration has occurred as a result of extreme weather events, along with associated damage to coastal infrastructure that has not been constructed to hurricane-proof standards.

4.2 Creating the enabling conditions to support blue growth

Growing the blue economy requires a range of framework conditions to be fulfilled, most obviously adequate infrastructure and highly skilled staff with access to low-skilled workers. Other essential conditions include: public acceptance, a solid legal framework regarding international waters and good governance at the local and regional levels. At the same time, it should be recognised that trade-offs will need to be made where space is limited and a combination of all activities is not feasible. Clear and co-ordinated institutional mechanisms for integrated coastal and ocean management established and implemented across relevant sectors such as fisheries, tourism, transport, energy, health and environment, will be essential to accommodate and resolve conflicts between the vast range of marine-related interests and values.

The successful and sustainable development of a blue economy will also require governance and policies that integrate environmental and economic considerations. The mix of marine resource development will be determined by existing governance structures, and will likely require new legislation, rules, strengthening of institutions and potentially the establishment of entirely new institutions. More importantly, translating new opportunities into productive sectors will require investment in research and development, building technical capacity, and creating the right environment to attract and retain outside investment. These have to be fundamental principles of the blue economy.

In order to fully realise the transition to a blue economy, the Commonwealth has identified seven key thematic areas (**enablers**) that are vital for creating the conditions for growth and investment. These enablers are not prioritised in order of importance and there are strong inter-relationships and synergies between them.

4.2.1 A healthy, resilient and productive marine environment

A key principle of the blue economy is that the health of the oceans is inextricably linked to the sustainability of economic livelihoods for coastal communities and the economy generally. As noted in section 1, the oceans also provide a range of essential goods and services that would be extremely costly to restore or replace once lost.

For SIDS, in particular, the health of coral reefs and associated biodiversity is of critical importance both from an environmental perspective and as an economic one, due to the strong reliance of SIDS' economies on the tourism and fisheries sectors. Thus, effective management of the marine environment and the maintenance and restoration of ecosystem health and integrity is fundamental to ecologically sustainable development.

4.2.2 Ocean governance

The existing ocean governance framework in most, if not all, SIDS emphasises a traditional sector-specific approach to management and planning, and thus shows symptoms of the problem facing a large number of countries seeking to implement a blue economy approach – ocean governance remains highly 'balkanised'. As governments encourage economic development of marine areas in the future, value-based conflict between competing interests is likely to increase. It will be difficult to resolve such conflicts without a more comprehensive and integrated approach to marine planning and decision-making, one which recognises the interactions and the interdependent nature of the various systems on islands.

Good governance and co-ordination across government is the unique key to achieving adequate management of the ocean and is, therefore, an overarching theme that is an essential part of the blue economy. A new approach is needed that recognises the full portfolio of possible uses and activities within the blue economy and therefore co-ordinates management across this portfolio (Commonwealth Secretariat, 2013a).

The overall aim of integrated governance arrangements should be to establish, strengthen and implement effective governance mechanisms that contribute to the implementation of the blue economy. Most, if not all, small states need to transition to a more integrated governance approach that requires all uses, users and values to be considered.

4.2.3 Business development, investment and finance

Many countries are developing and implementing strategic ocean development plans and policies to stimulate growth in their ocean space. These have the potential to significantly increase investment in and development of the blue economy (EIU 2015). Such strategic development plans focus on both existing sectors and new and emerging opportunities, such as those discussed in section 3.

The realisation of these opportunities will require strategies that:

- further support investment in and development of existing sectors;

- promote investment and innovation to support the development of new sectors, such as those discussed in section 3.5; and
- further develop the backward and forward linkages in the value chains of existing sectors.

According to the EIU (2015), '*many public and private economic activities that could serve to restore ocean health will carry higher up-front costs and returns that will not be immediately accrued to investors*'.

As such, in order to transition to a sustainable blue economy, it is also necessary to have in place *inter alia* sustainable financing mechanisms that will provide long-term and reliable funding to support blue economy activities, including conservation and sustainable management initiatives for marine and coastal resources, as well as the wider environment. A range of innovative finance mechanisms exist that could be applied to a range of initiatives, including fishery improvement projects, habitat restoration and protection projects, valorisation of a range of marine ecosystem service values, and projects that link coastal and marine ecosystems to climate change adaptation.

In SIDS, particularly, the greatest potential for value addition and job creation lies with the development of small and medium-sized enterprises within blue economy value chains. There is, therefore, a need to examine the mechanisms to encourage and finance start-up MSMEs and to assist with capacity and technology development.

4.2.4 Infrastructure

Coastal and port infrastructure are critical assets that serve as catalysts of economic growth and development in SIDS, since SIDS rely heavily on coastal tourism and are almost entirely dependent on maritime transport to facilitate global trade (UN Economic Commission for Africa [UNECA] 2014).

In many SIDS, tourism resorts, coastal towns and infrastructure are at risk, given their location at or near present sea level and their proximity to the coast. Relocation or fortifying coastal infrastructure for coastal protection will become financially burdensome for governments. Investment in coastal infrastructure improvements and a better-integrated approach to planning will afford the tools to help minimise hazards of flooding and erosion, and investments in coastal infrastructure and to optimise performance.

4.2.5 Technology, research and development

Research and development and other knowledge-generating activities: support sustainable economic growth and job creation through the development of new products and services; facilitate better management and protection of marine ecosystems; and inform policy, governance and regulation of the marine sector.

Knowledge of the marine environment is also a critical need for effective decision-making. The more that is known about the marine environment, the better people's interaction with it can be managed. Integrating diverse and complex information, supplemented by new research, contributes to the advancement and management of ocean resources.

Identifying and defining ongoing strategic marine research and information needs, in an inclusive and adaptive manner, together with the appropriate funding resources and mechanisms, is essential for achieving economic development through a blue economy framework.

4.2.6 Education and capacity building

A lack of education and training in many SIDS leads to chronic gaps in their technical capacity for marine research, planning and decision-making. Identifying future skills needs and labour market supply and demand trends, and adapting and developing existing education, vocational and professional training programmes to meet them, will be essential if the blue economy is to become a reality in SIDS.

A more co-ordinated focus between the existing research and educational facilities may well prove beneficial in terms of addressing key gaps in research skills and capacity building, but ultimately a more comprehensive research strategy is likely to be required if SIDS are to fully realise the opportunities presented by the blue economy.

4.2.7 Maritime surveillance, monitoring and enforcement

Creating the conditions needed for effective management of ocean space and future economic growth depends on an effective and efficient monitoring, surveillance and enforcement system.

The Commonwealth's experience of undertaking stakeholder engagement in several SIDS, for example, highlights the difficulties associated with the enforcement of existing rules and regulations, particularly with regard to fisheries. Although legal frameworks exist in most countries for many marine activities, there are often a number of regulatory gaps compared to the range of activities undertaken, as well as duplication between pieces of legislation addressing the same issue.

Of critical importance to future economic development is the fact that such frameworks often do not anticipate or provide an enabling environment for future uses of the marine environment. A further pressing concern is that current regulations are not enforced robustly in many countries.

A key element of monitoring and enforcement is surveillance of a nation's ocean space. Improving the procedures for monitoring and enforcement, and clearly defining the institutional and organisational responsibilities for the management of marine activities and resources between the various ministries and departments, is a crucial issue that must be addressed.

To this end, there is a need for small states to enhance their capability to identify threats to their maritime space in a timely manner by sharing and integrating intelligence, surveillance and navigation systems into a common operating picture to position decision-makers to prepare for, prevent, respond to and recover from a broad spectrum of potential maritime-related threats.

References

Commonwealth Secretariat (2013a), 'A New Approach to Ocean Governance: Practical ways to Fast Track the Green Economy', Commonwealth Discussion Paper No. 14, Commonwealth Secretariat, London, May 2013.

Economist Intelligence Unit (EIU) (2015), 'The Blue Economy: Growth, Opportunity and a Sustainable Ocean Economy', an Economist Intelligence Unit briefing paper for the World Ocean Summit 2015, available at: http://www.economistinsights.com/sites/default/files/Blue%20Economy_briefing%20paper_WOS2015.pdf (accessed on 21 March 2016).

UNCTAD (2014), *The Oceans Economy: Opportunities and Challenges for Small Island Developing States*, UNCTAD, Geneva.

UN Economic Commission for Africa (UNECA) (2014), *Unlocking the Full Potential of the Blue Economy: Are African Small Island Developing States Ready to Embrace the Opportunities?*, UNECA, Addis Ababa, available at: http://www.climdev-africa.org/sites/default/files/unsummit2014/Blue%20Economy%20-%20EN.pdf (accessed 26 April 2016).

Printed and bound by CPI Group (UK) Ltd, Croydon, CR0 4YY
14/07/2025
01915870-0001